Fisher-Price® Ready Readers

Stage 2 Grades 1-3

Dear Parents/Caregivers:

Children learn to read in stages, and all children develop reading skills at different ages. Ready Readers™ were created to encourage children's interest in reading and to increase their reading skills. Ready Readers™ stories are written on two levels to accommodate children ranging in grade level from preschool through third grade. These stages are meant to be used only as a guide.

Stage 1: Preschool–Grade 1

Stage 1 stories have short, simple sentences with large type. They are perfect for children who are getting ready to read or are just becoming familiar with reading on their own.

Stage 2: Grades 1–3

Stage 2 stories have longer sentences and are a bit more complex. They are suitable for children who are able to read but still may need help.

All of the Ready Readers™ stories are fun, easy-to-follow tales that are colorfully illustrated. The stories are arranged in a progressive order of difficulty. Children should read the stories in order to move from the simplest vocabulary and concepts to the most difficult within each stage. Reading will become an exciting adventure. Soon your child will not only be ready, but eager to read.

Educational Consultant: Mary McLean-Hely, M.A. Education: Design and Evaluation of Educational Programs, Stanford University

Contents

The Sleepover

Written by Nicole O'Neill
Illustrated by Art Mawhinney and Arthur Friedman

Cole's friend Sam is turning eight.

Sam is having a sleepover.
Cole can't wait!

It is time for Cole to pack.
What should he put into his sack?

He takes his toothbrush and
a comb.
He takes the things he uses
at home.

Cole has packed his bag just right.

He's seven and old enough to
stay out overnight!

Cole has never been to a
sleepover before.
Mom drops him off right at
Sam's door.

Mom tells Cole to give her
a call.
"I'll be fine," says Cole. "Don't
worry at all."

13

Cole has never slept away
from home.
Will he be all right on his own?

Cole sees that all of his friends
are here.
Everything is OK. He has no
fear!

Sam's mom made a
dinosaur cake.

Jeff ate too much.
He got a bellyache!

17

Cole and his friends laugh
and play.

Sam had a really great birthday!

Now it's time to turn out the light.

"Oh, no," thinks Cole. "Will I be all right?"

What's that noise? What's that sound?

What's this beast that Cole
has found?

It is a little bit scary
without any light.

Cole goes to the kitchen
to get a bite.

Cole hears a lot of noise.

In the kitchen, he sees
all the boys!

27

"I was thirsty," says Cole's friend, Ron.

"Um, I was too," says Ron's twin, Jon.

All of his friends feel the same.

Cole doesn't feel any shame!

Now the sun is shining bright.

Cole made it through the night!

"Were you scared?" asks Mom, later that day.

"A little bit, Mom," says Cole. "But everything turned out OK!"

Tabby's Team

Written by Nicole O'Neill

Illustrated by Art Mawhinney

I'm going to try out for a team.

To be an athlete is my dream.

I'll practice hard. I'll sweat. I'll train.

I can play any game!

The baseball team seems like fun.

So, over to the field I run.

We have practice every day.

I can't wait to really play.

Today is our very first game.

On my new uniform is my name!

The ball is coming! It's almost here!

I didn't catch it. But I hear a cheer.

"No sweat, Tappy," says Coach Ted.

"Telly caught the ball instead."

Now I step up to the plate.

My swing missed. It was too late.

"That's OK," says Coach Ted.

"Tubby scored. We're still ahead."

But I want to score a run.

Otherwise, it's just no fun!

Coach says that's not what a team is about.

We have to help each other out.

We will cheer when you score.

That's what a baseball team is for.

My next time up I hit the ball.

It goes all the way to the wall!

Playing baseball is just great.
And the best part is my teammates!

A Pet for Us

Written by Nicole O'Neill

Illustrated by Scott Earle

We are getting a pet!
Mom says we ALL have
to agree on what kind of
pet to get.

Alex wants a snake.
Julia does not like snakes.
You can't walk a snake.

So, no snake for us!

Julia wants a turtle. Anthony thinks that turtles are no fun. You can't take a nap with one.

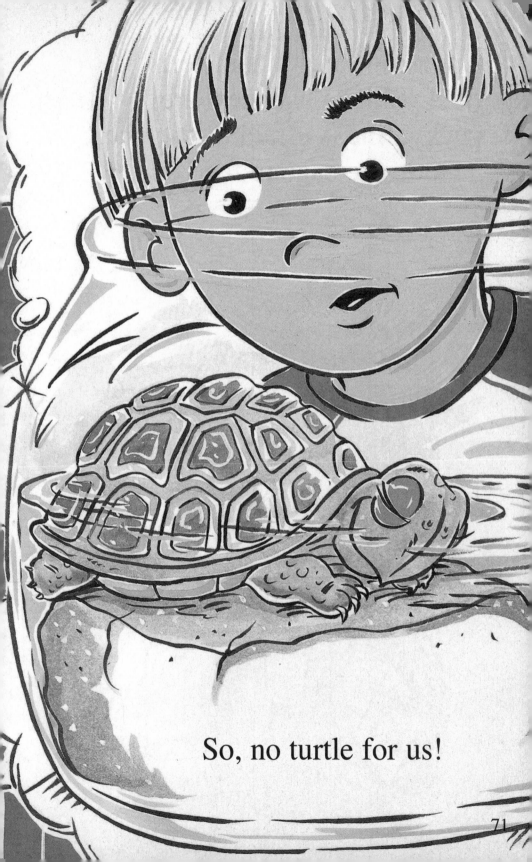

So, no turtle for us!

Anthony wants a hamster.
Becky thinks hamsters are
yucky. She is afraid to stick her
hand in the cage to feed one.

So, no hamster for us!

Becky wants a giraffe.
I explain that it is hard to give
a giraffe a bath.

So, no giraffe for us!

I want a fish. Alex says that a fish can't run around and play.

So, no fish for us!

We can't agree on anything!
We'll never get a pet.

Mom and Dad take us to the
pet store.

Alex likes the bunnies.

Julia likes the birds.

Becky likes the kittens.

Anthony likes the lizards.
No one can agree!

Then we see a small puppy.
He wags his tail at us.

That's how we all know that
he is perfect.

The puppy is our new pet!
His new name is Mugsy.

Julia walks Mugsy.

Anthony takes naps
with Mugsy.

Becky feeds him.

I give Mugsy his bath.

Alex likes to run and play
with Mugsy.

We love our new pet.
Finally—something
we agree on!

Jill's Glasses

Written by Nancy Parent

Illustrated by Phyllis Harris

One day when Jill Bloom
went to school,

Be considerate

of others.

she couldn't read the
classroom rule.

Jill thought her eyes were getting worse.

She went to see Miss Patch,
the nurse.

Jill read the chart and thought that "E" came right after the letter "C."

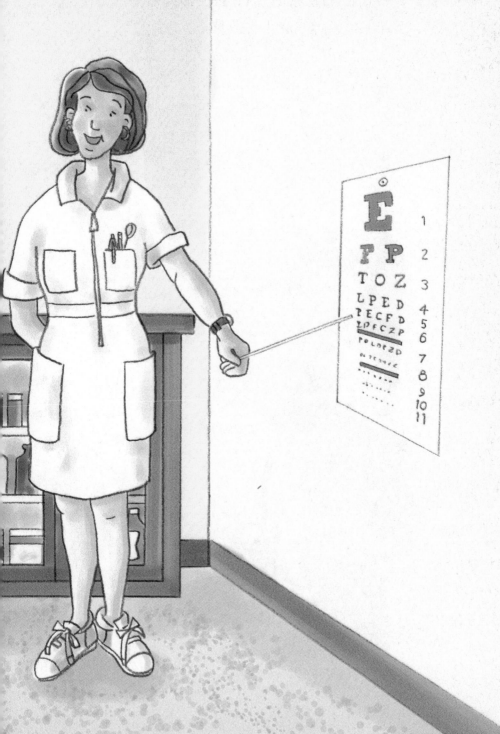

So Jill got glasses right away.

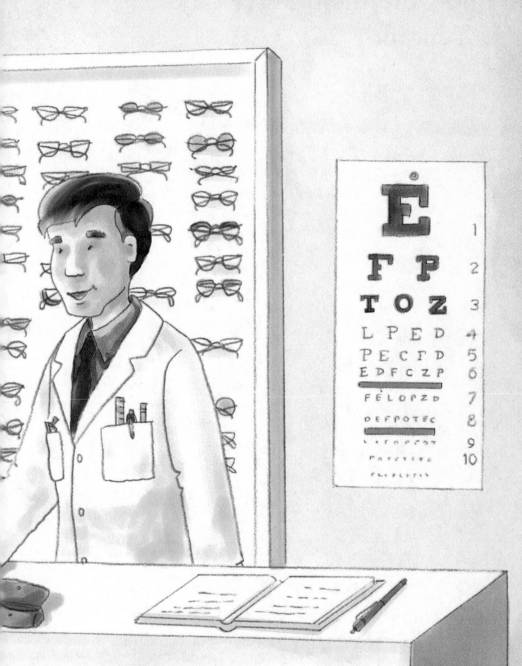

She put them on and cried,
"Hooray!"

She wore them every day
at school.

The other kids thought
she was cool.

Be considerate of others.

Jill felt so happy,
she cried, "Look!"

"Now I can read my science book!"

Why, Jill could see the
soccer ball,

and the goalie standing tall.

Jill wore glasses in the sun.

Wearing them was really fun.

She kept her glasses on in bed.
"Please take them off," her
mother said.

But Jill was falling fast asleep.
She never even heard a peep.

When Jill woke up, she couldn't see.

Where, oh, where could her glasses be?

Jill looked high, and Jill looked low. But where they were, she didn't know.

She had to hurry or be late.
The school bus wasn't going
to wait.

Jill ran and got right on the bus.

The driver didn't make a fuss.

She quickly found an
empty seat.

She almost tripped on
someone's feet.

She sat down next to her friend Ted, who found Jill's glasses on her head!

Sir Charmer, the Brave

Written by Nancy Parent

Illustrated by Pulsar Studio

Andrew's class was putting on a play.

"Sir charmer, the Brave"

It was called
"Sir Charmer,
the Brave."

"Everyone will play a part," said his teacher, Ms. Jones.

"Who will be Prince Sloppy,
and who will be Princess Neat?"

125

"Then there's the dragon,"
she continued.
"Now let me see. Would you like
that part, Howard Lee?"

When Ms. Jones
was through,
everyone had
a part except
for Andrew.

Andrew quickly raised his hand. "What about me?" he asked.

Ms. Jones smiled.
"You can be Sir Charmer,
the brave knight."

Andrew's class read the script for the play.

"This is going to be fun!" he thought. But first he had to learn his lines.

Andrew's favorite part was the duel with Prince Sloppy.

He even got to tame a fire-breathing dragon.

Nothing scared Sir Charmer. Nothing that is…until opening night.

On opening night, Andrew
peeked through the curtains and
saw a lot of people.

His teeth started chattering.
Andrew had a bad case of
stage fright.

The play was about to start, but
Andrew couldn't move.

"Places everyone!" called
Ms. Jones.

Andrew shook his head. He just
couldn't go out there.

"Take a deep breath," Ms. Jones said. "I'm going to count to ten and open the curtain."

When the curtain opened, Andrew looked out at the audience. He saw his parents smiling proudly.

Andrew cleared his throat and began:

"Welcome to our little show,
It's about the knights of long ago.
If there's a need, I'll lend a hand.
I'm the bravest knight in all the land."

A Special Week

Written by Nicole O'Neill

Illustrated by Jewel Mitchell

I am going on a trip.

I am going to visit Grandma Jean
and Grandpa Dom.

I get to spend a whole entire week with them! We do lots of fun stuff together.

I have my own room at
Grandma's house.

It used to be my mom's room
when she was a little girl.

Grandma loves the picture
I made for her.

"It's beautiful, my little chickie-doo," she says. She always calls me her little chickie-doo!

Grandpa tells me lots of stories
about the good old days.
His stories are the best.

Grandpa and I like to go on picnics and wiggle our toes in the grass.

I help Grandma wash her car.

Grandma and Grandpa have
lots of old pictures.

That's my uncle and my mom
when they were young.

Grandpa lets me stay up past
my bedtime. We watch
television together. He's my pal.

Grandma brushes my hair when it gets tangled. She makes pretty braids.

Grandpa and Grandma have a
great big garden. I get to pick
any flower I want!

Grandpa takes me to get
ice cream.

He lets me get three scoops—
with sprinkles!

I am Grandma's special
little helper.

Grandpa and I go for a walk.

When I get tired, he puts me
on his shoulders.

When it's time for bed,
Grandma reads me a story.

She knows all of my favorites!

I love Grandma and Grandpa!
I can't wait to come back!

Patrick's Castle

Written by Ellen Hawley

Illustrated by Una Fricker, Artful Doodlers

"Do you want to help me build my castle?" Patrick asked Andy.

"No," Andy said.

"We can make it really big,"
replied Patrick.

"No. I'll help you later," Patrick's big brother said. "See how big you can build it by yourself."

"Okay. Later," Patrick thought, resting his head on his knees.

When Patrick looked up, his castle was finished.

A boy was leading a horse
across the drawbridge.

185

"Prince Patrick, hurry!" the boy said. "A dragon's attacking the village. You must save it."

"Prince?" Patrick said. "Dragon? Me?"

Patrick rode down the beach
to find the dragon.

Patrick drew his sword.

"Dragon!" he called.

The dragon roared, "Are you going to fight me with that little toothpick?"

"If I have to," replied Patrick.
The dragon laughed so hard that
fire spit out of its nose.

193

But Patrick walked up to the dragon and laid his sword on its tail.

"Dragon fine, claw and scale, you're mine because I touched your tail," he chanted.

"Now go away," Patrick said.

The dragon roared. It breathed fire.
But then it flew away.

The villagers ran to Patrick.
They cheered and danced.

"I beat the dragon all by myself,"
thought Patrick.

All of a sudden Patrick woke up.

Andy was sitting next to him.
He had built the best sandcastle
that Patrick ever saw.

"Where have you been?" asked
Andy. "I had to build this castle
all by myself."

"Wow! Thanks, Andy," Patrick said.

"Let's play knights and dragons or something," Andy said. Patrick smiled. "Or something," he said.

The Adventures of Lily and Daisy

Written by Jacqueline Zurawski

Illustrated by Liz Goulet Dubois

Lily and Daisy are sweet
little flowers.

They stand in the sunshine for
hours and hours.

Standing all day makes them tired.

They have nothing to do but
be sniffed and admired.

They look pretty and show off their petals.

They try to be patient until nighttime settles.

Then they pull up their roots—ouch, that smarts.

With playful smiles the
adventure starts.

Tonight they decide to
go to the park.

Only the moonbeams
light up the dark.

They sneak to the park and
shout with glee.

There's so much to do and
so much to see.

They play in the sandbox the way they see children play in it day after day.

They climb a ladder and
go down a slide.

It's long and twisted and,
wow, what a ride!

Then on to the swings—they swing so high.

They think their roots might
touch the sky!

The climbers are great fun
to climb.

They had so much fun that
they lost track of time.

The moonlight no longer shows
the way.

The colors in the sky mark the start of a new day.

They make it back safely to
their holes in the ground.

They plop down their roots and tuck them in safe and sound.

Lily and Daisy had a night
filled with fun!

They found
sand and swings
and a place to run.

231

Another long day and no
adventures in sight—at least,
they agree, until tonight.

Best Friends

Written by Susan Wallach

Illustrated by Paul E. Nunn

Becca and I have been best friends forever.

We have fun together.
Sometimes we pretend
we're sisters!

We love bubble gum and Halloween.

Last year we were mermaids.

We don't like monsters!

But we love our clubhouse.

We think my new brother
James is cute, but noisy.

Because of him, my mother is too tired to plan my birthday party.

Instead of a party, Becca and I will have a sleepover.

We'll stay up all night and
wear my mother's old gowns.

We both think my older
sister Alice is bossy.

She gets everything she wants.
She has her own phone and stereo.

Becca and I never hang out
with Alice. She's always too
busy doing grown-up things.

Becca and I think
Alice is silly.

But, lately, Becca wants to talk to Alice when she calls.

They meet after school, whispering and giggling.

My sister has everything and
now she has my best friend!

I have no one to play with after
school. Becca is too busy being
Alice's best friend.

Worst of all, my birthday is
tomorrow. How can I have a
sleepover without a friend to
sleep over?

My family gives me gifts, but I don't care because Becca isn't my best friend anymore.

I don't care that my father takes me to the zoo to see the baby ostrich.

I don't care that nobody's home when we return.

"Surprise!" Becca and Alice
have been planning my surprise
birthday party all week.

259

But the best present is that Becca and I are still best friends!

Howard's Screechy Violin

Written by Nancy Parent

Illustrated by Jilly Slattery

One day, Howard decided he wanted to play the violin. He went to see his music teacher at school.

"You must practice every day,"
she said.

That night, Howard took out
his violin and began to play.

His violin made lots of screechy
sounds. It scared his cat, Jack.
It made his dog, Sam, cry.

"Bye!" called Matt, his older brother, running for the door.

"I think I left something in
the car," said Howard's dad.
His little sister, Molly, crawled
under the table.

The next night, the babysitter
came over.

When Howard played, she put
her headphones over her ears.

But Howard's mother loved to hear him play.

She even clapped when he was done.

Every night, after dinner,
Howard practiced his violin.

And every night, his brother,
sister, dad, and pets all ran
away.

"Where do you think they go?"
asked Howard.
His mom just shrugged.

One night, Howard's family got tired of running away.

"Well," said Mom. "I always say...
if you can't beat him, join him!"

"How?" asked Molly. "None of us can play the violin."

"What instrument can you play?"
asked Mom.

"I can play the tambourine!"
cried Molly.

"I can play the clarinet," said Matt.

"I can play the guitar," said Dad.

"I can play the piano," said
Mom.

The next night, the whole family played together.
After a few weeks, they sounded really good—even Howard!

Mrs. Tumble and the babysitter joined in.

Howard and his family held a concert for the neighbors.

Everyone loved it!

Howard's family became known
as Howard Clark and His Musical
Larks. They played at parties,
picnics, and on holidays.

And it all started with
Howard's screechy violin.